G000125182

A SPIRITUAL
JOURNAL

Also by Toby Negus

The Sacred you – How to be your own saviour

The heart knows what the mind cannot see

A SPIRITUAL
JOURNAL

*This book is my spiritual journal, it contains the pictures
and descriptions of the essence understandings that have
been accumulated during 40 years of exploration into the
meaning of life and the how and why we do what we do.*

"Toby Negus is an artist, both with paints and of the spirit. His work reflects a deep commitment to meeting life on its terms and an equally deep understanding of human nature. I appreciate the gentleness and empathy with which he approaches fellow humans in his writings"

Jacob Nordby - author of *The Divine Arsonist* and *Blessed Are the Weird - A Manifesto for Creatives.*

"A beautiful and soulful book of wisdom, inspired art, radiant colour and prose, encouraging us to embody both the light and the shadow, the conscious and the unconscious, while supporting the creative essence of who were born to be. Toby encourages us to live our joy, and reminds us that we have the capacity to design our lives and choose how to live each day! Truly, this book is a lovely celebration for healing the heart and nurturing the soul."

Heather McCloskey Beck – International speaker and author of *Take the Leap*

ACKNOWLEDGEMENT

I would like to acknowledge all the great
teachers of my life, both known and unknown,
seen and unseen.

Above all I would like to acknowledge my heart
who, when I have allowed it, has given me an
endless supply of intelligence and love.

DEDICATION

This book is dedicated to you the reader that
you may find and live the life you love.

CONTENTS

TOBY NEGUS

What a story I am, so much has made me who I am. So many tunes have I heard, so many songs have I sung, so many dances have I danced. A kaleidoscope of life.

Its almost bizarre and yet...
There has always been me,
the person living the story!

It does not make sense to the sensible mind,
it is just way too much.
So I must conclude
that the understanding of who I am
is beyond my perception.

That being so,
I must resign my grasp on who I think I am,
allow the pen to tell me the story,
the brush to paint the picture,

and the soul to sing the song.

A B O U T   T H I S B O O K

This book is a collection of pictures and words that I have created in response to an insatiable urge to understand myself and the world.

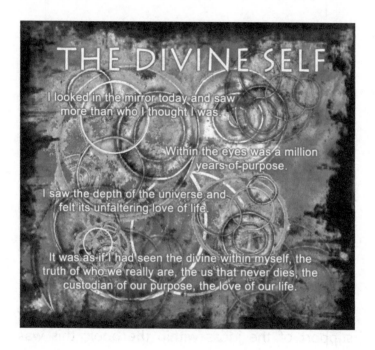

THE DIVINE SELF

I looked in the mirror today and saw more than who I thought I was.

Within the eyes was a million years of purpose.

I saw the depth of the universe and felt its unfaltering love of life.

It was as if I had seen the divine within myself, the truth of who we really are, the us that never dies, the custodian of our purpose, the love of our life.

I've always loved colour and the power of images and always have written down the meanings that I have gleaned from life. So it seemed natural to put them together, to draw an image for my thoughts or to write words for an image.

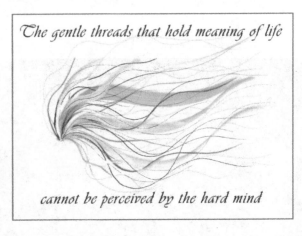

The gentle threads that hold meaning of life

cannot be perceived by the hard mind

My art creations began seriously when I wrote my first book 'The Sacred You'. I wanted to have images to support the writing and had to decide if I was going to use other people's artwork or create my own. I decided that it should be mine, so I began to create a whole set of images in support of the ideas within the book; this was tough and I had to work through 'this is impossible' many, many times. But it really started my art life in earnest.

Much of my art is driven by the desire to express an idea or concept that I find powerful and wish to embed in myself and share with others. One of the first artworks I did was about the importance of not being timid with the loves we feel about life. I felt this timidity in myself and saw it in most people I met – this was not good! The loves we feel about life are so, so important in releasing our dream and finding the core of ourselves.

The image I drew was of some flowers that looked so bold and I really loved the colour of. It was one of my first artworks and took a lot of courage to do. It looked a bit crude but that was okay because it was honest and heartfelt and that was part of the point.

THE JOURNEY

Advice to my younger self for his spiritual journey.

You are going on a journey to heal the heart and free the mind. It is a journey of remembering the truth of who you already are.

What should I pack for the journey?
The heart, openness and passion. The heart because it holds the purpose and the light. Openness because the journey cannot be what you expect. Passion because it will open the gates of your mind.

Who will I meet on the way?
In your journey to self you will only meet one person, but they will have a thousand faces. Be kind to all for they are you.

What the weather will be like on the journey?
There will be sunny days and rainy days, days that will warm the soul and days that you may never have wished for, but after they have passed, they will be thanked for the light that they gave.

6

What will I be doing on the journey?
On the journey you will craft beautiful gems from your passion of life. Some will be crafted in the dark, others in the light, all will shine, all will bring light to the world.

What will I get from the journey?
On the journey you will remember more of you really are, and as this sense grows so will the compassion that you feel for your self. This compassion will, in time, spread to all that you see.

What are the pitfalls that I may encounter?
The only pitfall is what is opposite to love and that is fear. It will have many guises but they will all have the same purpose, to make you closed and to move you away from your heartfelt feelings about life.

What is a good reminder for the journey?
Remember that you are not a human learning to be spiritual but a spirit learning to be human. There is a difference: one embraces humanity, the other does not.

CHOICE

I CHOOSE WHAT I WILL FEEL

Whatever this day means for me is my choice.

I can, if I wish, give it any meaning that I want.

It will not change the day but it will change me.

THE SACRED YOU

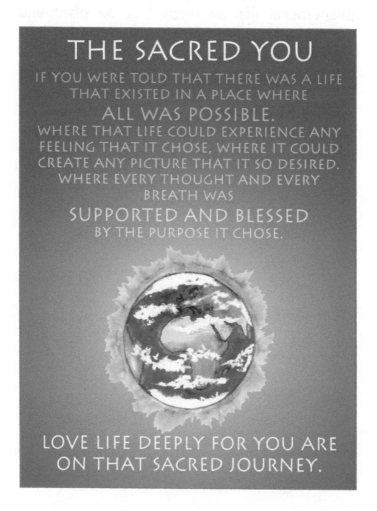

THE SACRED YOU

IF YOU WERE TOLD THAT THERE WAS A LIFE
THAT EXISTED IN A PLACE WHERE
ALL WAS POSSIBLE.
WHERE THAT LIFE COULD EXPERIENCE ANY
FEELING THAT IT CHOSE, WHERE IT COULD
CREATE ANY PICTURE THAT IT SO DESIRED.
WHERE EVERY THOUGHT AND EVERY
BREATH WAS
SUPPORTED AND BLESSED
BY THE PURPOSE IT CHOSE.

LOVE LIFE DEEPLY FOR YOU ARE
ON THAT SACRED JOURNEY.

We are sacred-worthy of spiritual respect.

We live within the domain of the earth, a place of phenomenal life; all seeds that we plant and nurture will grow, it cannot *not* happen because it is the way of this place, to lend her power to all intentions that we make.

And we have within our mind and our heart the will and passion to create any purpose for our life, to follow any dream we choose.

I CHOOSE WHAT
I WILL DO

I N N E R C H I L D

We are the guardian angel of the family
of ourselves. The consciousness of all
the unknown memories of our lives.

*It's easy to love myself when I am feeling
good; it's tricky when I am feeling bad and
it can seem impossible when I am feeling
ugly.*

We do not love the grumpy of us, the sad of us, the hostile of ourselves, the parts of us that act as if we do not care. We name them as 'not us' and so drive a sword into ourselves, separating ourselves into the good and the bad, the worthy and the unworthy of ourselves. We declare a part of ourselves as a 'disturber of the peace', a foe to our purpose, an antagonist to our harmony, and so we become the intolerant parent to the hurting child within us, the part in us that is in distress, in need of understanding, in need of love.

Every day on this planet

There are so many caring thoughts being given.

There is so much willingness happening.

There is so much joy being felt.

There are so many acts of kindness offered.

There is so much warmth being shared.

There is so much hope being felt.

There is so much courage being generated.

There is so much love being made known.

Rejoice in the life we are

Every moment on this planet there are a thousand thousand acts being created that bring light and warmth into the world.

13

The world is full of so much more than what we are told, so much more than the images of pain and hostility that are shown in the media. Every moment of every day there are so many people doing so many things that bring light to the world. Every day there are people who inspire youth to fulfil their dreams, artists who create wonders that make us smile, dance and wonder at the beauty of life. Every day there are people who are going into the dark places of the world to bring kindness and light, and every day thousands of ordinary, extraordinary people are getting up with courage to face another day despite the pains that they feel. Every day thousands of people are giving a smile or a hug that does so much for another. And every day thousands of people put aside their own problems and share their tenderness. There really are so many people doing so many things that bring brightness to the world. God bless them!

ITS OK TO BE YOU

To Love Yourself
means
it's OK to be you

*I do shy away from being myself, as if I fear
that I am not enough, not strong enough to
be who I really am.*

But this is only an illusion created by the ghosts of the media and our way of life. They do haunt the mind with their cries of 'more' always more, before we can feel settled, before we can be happy, before we can be ourselves.

But really it's OK to be you; there is no one else to be nor anything else needed to be who you are. You are, were and always will be enough.

Who you are is important; it's taken your lifetime to create. The tears, the laughter, the love have created a unique soul that is like no other. If the truth be told, it is that you are very special and when you are at peace with yourself, you know this to be true.

We have been given the ability to create pictures in our mind with all the sensations of reality, to imagine anything that we wish.

But we have been led to believe that imagination is for children and does not belong in the real world. This myth has been created so we don't play havoc with the ordered money making machines of the world. So they give us the imagination of the glossy pages to keep us away from knowing the greater truths of our life.

Our imagination is a window to other worlds, worlds of immeasurable colour and possibility, of pictures that defy our expectations. It gives us connection to stories we have only ever dreamed of and landscapes of infinite beauty. It is a magic power of creativity that allows us to build bridges between what is and what can be.

We are truly the magician and our imagination is our wand of command.

THE POWER AND
VISION OF THE DREAM

COMES FROM THE
HEART OF
OURSELVES

*The power and vision of the dream comes
from the heart of me.*

So I must divine my own heart to be able to hear its song and allow myself to dance its meaning.

My heart is the chamber of my deepest feelings about life. It is the earth from where all beauty is made manifest. The journey back to the heart of me is my life's journey, because when I touch my heart, I rejoin life at its very core and become a celebration of all that I hold dear.

Everyone wants to be happy; it guides our lives. But the world would have me believe that life is a struggle for the resources that are needed before I can be happy, that there is not enough time, money or love to be happy now. So I wait to be happy with the lists of the things I need before I can decide that I am happy – the 'I will be happy when' list and the 'if only' list.

So I give up being happy to be and do things in order to be happy!

We do have a preset level of happiness according to how worthy we think we are. But that level of happiness is only in our imagination and can be changed at any time by our decision to be happier now; despite whatever may or may not be happening in our lives, we can decide to up our level of happiness, to declare to our grumpy or sad self that we are OK. We can still be sad or grumpy but it will be an OK sad or an OK grumpy.

When we do this we let go of our assumptions about ourselves and tap into the reservoir of light within ourselves; our world then becomes brighter because of it.

We don't need a reason to be happy only our decision to be so.

SELF INTEGRITY

Each time we withhold our truth
withhold our light
or withhold our love
we abandon who we really are

There are many times in a day when we
choose who we will be in our response to life.

There are many times in a day when I choose who I will be in my response to life, in my response to the people and things that happen upon or within me. What part of me will take the stage, give a speech or do an action? And there are so many aspects of me: the timid, brave, the hostile, the fearful, the loving; they are all waiting in the wings for their time upon the stage.

But if I let go of my truth for the sake of appeasement, doubt my value and hide my light or withhold my love for fear of seeming childish, I no longer respond to the true script of me and break the integrity of myself. I separate myself from the part of me that holds my purpose in life and become an act of pale imitation to the true colours of life.

This is not a call to be belligerent to life but rather to cherish the heart and the truth of ourselves above all things because we know that without them, there is no life.

24

I CHOOSE WHO
I AM

As soon as I think myself lesser or greater
than another,

I claim the truth to be outside of me.

This is neither wise, true nor useful.

DREAMS

We are far more than we think we are, and the dreams that we carry about our life connect us to this greater us. They not only bring meaning to our life, they are the meaning of our life. And in our journey to breathe life into them, we honour the deeper promise we made to ourselves for this lifetime.

N O W   I S
E N O U I G H

We are pulled out of the now into our tomorrow or our yesterdays, as if now were not enough.

I am dragged away from the now by asking 'what does it mean?' As if it could mean anything but everything.

I let slip the moment of the now by insisting that I be in the picture as if I are not already there.

I am enticed into the moment yet to come as if it has the answers to the moment I am already in.

Now is enough because it is everything; it is only my fragile self that fears the enormity of the now and likes to fix and secure things with thoughts of what if and what was.

We don't have to wait to be who we are. We are, were and always will be enough.'

OUR REASON WHY

What we plant
as our reasons 'why'

*grow to become the feelings
of who we are*

Our sense of self— 'who we think we are' —
has been created from the thousands of 'why
we do what we do.' These are the messages
we have told ourselves about who we are
and who we wish to be.

Of all the powers we have been given, our ability to choose why we do what we do is the most profound; it is the light and the beacon that guides our destiny. It is the causal essence of our actions; what is behind the smile, the handshake or when we treat ourselves to a little something. They create the energy and the signal we are sending to ourselves and the world about who we are. And when we do listen, the motives we create become the sign posts that guide our instincts and our mind, they become the background noise that we identify as ourselves.

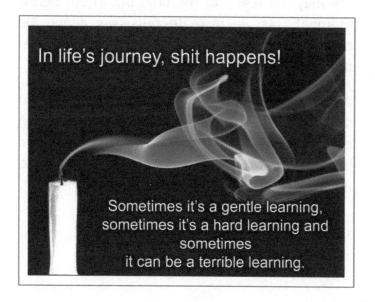

In life's journey, shit happens!

Sometimes it's a gentle learning,
sometimes it's a hard learning and
sometimes
it can be a terrible learning.

When life's experiences cause us a terrible learning, extinguishing our very grasp on who we think we are, we can find ourselves alone, in the dark, crawling on the broken shards of all that we were. We are driven into the core of our life to find the will to raise ourselves in the face of what appears an impossible weight.

We may not feel it at the time but in our heroic moments, as we recreate ourselves anew, the purpose and the dedication we create touches the very heart of life.

Although it is a learning that we would wish on no other, it leaves us with a profound gift, for in our endeavour to heal the pain, we craft a beautiful gem that has no comparison and the universe grows because of its presence.

Talk gently to yourself about

what you truly care about.

So you will know

who you really are.

When I speak to myself in harsh terms, without compassion, I do not talk to myself, I talk *at* myself, alienating a part of me as 'not me' and making an enemy of my very self.

33

The deeper of me can't always understand the shouting and the careless conversation I give myself about things that mean nothing to the heart of me. But if I share my dreams, my hopes and my loves with myself, and talk gently to myself about what I truly care about, that part of me does listen and it so wishes to be part of this great adventure of life.

When I share my heart's wishes with myself
I build a communion that allows me to
cherish and be cherished by the light of who
I really am.

T R U S T

Trust that there is a part of you that
loves you dearly

TRUST

Trust that when you are at peace
with yourself you will know that
you are not alone

*Although I live in a world of this and that,
there is within me, dreams of forever and
the memories of the infinite.*

I do live two lives: the ordinary one, that is full of the this and that I have to do to make ends meet, to keep my heart sound and bring opportunities for happiness into my life. And I have my extraordinary life, the life when my spirits soar, my mind is set free and my heart becomes healed by the presence of my loved purpose. When I am in this life, I know that I am loved and trust that everything is actually OK. But on my return to the ordinary life, as I scramble again for the this and that, I can lose the sense of trust that I felt in my extraordinary life and become blind again to my loved purpose.

This is how it must be, this back and forth, but I can choose to remember to remember that there is a part of me that loves me dearly, which holds the trust that everything is actually OK.

MEMORIES

*Do not describe yourself with your
memories, you are so much more.
Do not describe where you are with your
memories, it is so much more.*

I am more than who I think am, far more;
whenever I let go of my memories and touch the
moment of the now, two universes meet. I
become a part of all that I see, and the view is
breathtaking.

I CHOOSE THE TRUTH I SPEAK

I always do our best but sometimes do not forgive myself for not being perfect.

Each day we start again, give our best, try with our heart to be the person we love to be. We never stop. We never do less than our best – it may have been a misinformed best or even a grumpy best, but it was always our best at the time.

We can't *not* try, with who we are in the moment, to be what we love. It's been the story of our extraordinary life and we should forgive ourselves for any hurt we have done to ourselves because of who we thought we should have been but were not.

We can always be better, stronger, wiser, brighter, more loving. Without the wish to be so we would never grow in ourselves, but when that wish turns sour, ceases to be the inspiration and becomes the tyrant to ourselves, we cast out our love and dismember ourselves, laying waste our peace and well-being.

To forgive ourselves is to bring to the light a part of ourselves that we have orphaned by our hostility. It makes whole the family of ourselves, giving us back the peace and strength that can only come from a unified self.

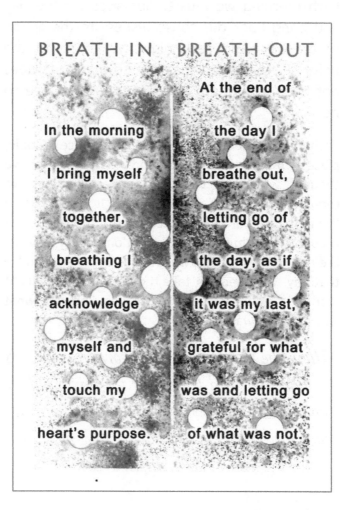

BREATH IN   BREATH OUT

	At the end of
In the morning	the day I
I bring myself	breathe out,
together,	letting go of
breathing I	the day, as if
acknowledge	it was my last,
myself and	grateful for what
touch my	was and letting go
heart's purpose.	of what was not.

Each morning I muster myself for the day and each night I let go of the universe I have created.

41

Each morning we muster ourselves for the day and bring back our consciousness to the action of the day. And each night we let go of the universe we created that day, so that what does not belong may slip away and leave us free to be.

Each day we meet a universe of experience: people, places, memories, hopes and fears, things we thought would be but were not and things we thought were not, that were. It really is a kaleidoscope of experience with thousands of thoughts and hundreds of emotions every day. At the end of the day, it is what it was and is enough for that day. We need not take the day into the twilight worlds of sleep; let go of what was, knowing what was of value, was valued.

Allow the grace of sleep to work its wonders upon us. And trust that the dawn will again, as it always has, present us with a new day empty of what was, save what we choose to bring into it.

Every
step we
take

creates
life.

*Every step we take is filled with the purpose
of our moment, and every day a thousand
sparks are created by our life.*

*A moment does not go by without us
creating life, be it in a look, a smile,
a thought.*

*Every moment of every day we are doing it.
We cannot stop; it is how we are
made to be.*

*This power of creation is a phenomenal gift,
for we may choose any purpose
for any step we take.*

BLAME

We do justify our attitudes by
blaming other people for who
we are.

*If I am not blaming other people and things
for how I am feeling, I turn this blame
upon myself, causing me to go to war with
my very self.*

We do justify our grumpy attitudes by blaming others for who we are. By doing this we give away the authority of who we are to other people and things, and so avoid the truth of ourselves, alienating our self from our own will and self-worth. But the most dangerous blame that we do is to ourselves.

When our emotions are supporting us in being who we wish to be, they are great. But when our feelings drive us away from who we wish to be, it's easy to use blame as a relief from the emotions we have made. But to hurt ourselves with blame only scares our beauty and pushes happiness further from our mind.

This can be shameful and drain the hope from our life. It stigmatises a part of ourselves as not us, causing us to go to war with our very self.

REAL LEARNING

REAL LEARNING IS NOT
WHAT WE EXPECT

IF WE COULD EXPECT IT
WOULD NOT BE LEARNING

*I carry many expectations and conditions of
how things should be; what the next day
will be, next year, even the next moment is
crowded before I get there, with the feelings
and meanings I think it will give.*

Although my expectations and conditions do give me a sense of security, it does make my actual moments a shadow of the real thing with little or no real learning.

Real self-learning seems to be reserved for those unexpected times, times when the light manages to shine through the wall of my expectations and conditions of how I think things should be. And although this light can often be shocking to who I think I am, it always offers bridges to the miraculous of who I can be.

YOU ARE NEVER ALONE

When you are at peace with yourself

Life can be strange; I can sometimes feel alone amongst people and sometimes not alone, graced with a presence, when I am just with myself.

So who is this part of me that can appear and make me feel comforted, supported and loved?

Whenever I settle in myself, stop the outward search for who I think I am, the illusion that something is missing evaporates and is replaced with a knowing that I am OK, are enough.

I cease my challenge to me and befriend myself again, allowing the presence of myself to return. This power I feel, is the truth of me and it is precious, connecting me to the flow of life. It is never truly absent, but I do wander off so easily, leaving myself bereft of its companionship.

When I am quiet enough to hear the whisper of my soul,
I am reminded of all that I hold dear,
all that I love and all that loves me.

Within the eyes
of all
can be seen
the child
of the
universe.

Within the eyes of all can be seen the child of the universe, the spirit that lives in the moment, is in awe of the enormity of life and never stops looking for ways to express its love of life.

51

It is who we knew when we were very young and it never leaves us.

I may act like a grown up and strut and fret about this and that but this is not the truth of myself. it is but a grey mantle I wear that hides the colours of my true nature.

Self love can be tough because we have to be soft to the parts of us that make us hard.

The mind does not listen to
what we are thinking

The Mind

it listens to why we are thinking it

*The mind does not keep all the thoughts we
have, that is far to cumbersome for it; it
leaves that to the brain to hold the memory
of our thoughts.*

The mind gets its power from holding onto the cause of our thoughts, the 'why' we are thinking them. These essences are what constitute the minds power and they become the persuasion it gives back to the thinking as to what to think about, what avenues to take in its chamber of possible associations of 'what goes with what'; for we do think different thoughts about the same thing according to how we are feeling that day.

The mind is the director of our thoughts, But to know what direction to give them, it listens to the reason why we are thinking about what we are thinking, the reason why we think about a person, place or thing. It looks to discern the causal essence, be it fear, love, greed, care; whatever it is, its job is to then to remind the thinking of what it has told it is important.

All is now

The stream of life and its truth exists in the moment of the now, not in tomorrow, yesterday or the next moment.

Now is all

There is only now. I may live away from the moment by my thoughts of its meaning or by comparing it to other moments, but this moment of now is all there really is and it is unique.

All is OK

Despite my insistence sometimes that things may not be OK, they are nevertheless, what is. And that means that what is is tangible, changeable, learn from-able; that I am in the picture, in the place of action, in life. And that is always OK.

CHOICES

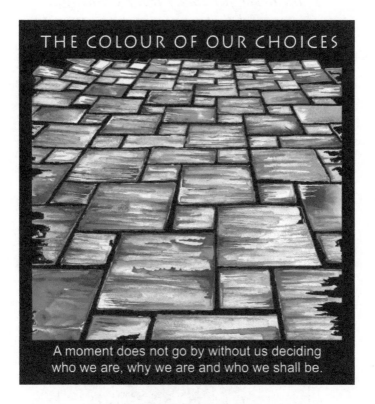

THE COLOUR OF OUR CHOICES

A moment does not go by without us deciding
who we are, why we are and who we shall be.

We choose what face to give to the world and
what response to give to our feelings. We decide
how much we smile and how much we cry, what
we fear and what we love. A moment does not
go by without us deciding who we are, why we
are and who we shall be. Each and every step we
take brings us the colour of our choices

*I am never far away from creating a
communion with the source of life. Breaking
the illusion that I am alone and reuniting
our consciousness to the stream of life.
It is never really far away it's only my
thought that it is, that makes it so.*

A THOUGHT CAN
CHANGE THE WORLD

Our will to express
our loves

is a sacred thread

that leads to the very core
of our existence.

*We have, within the very heart of ourselves,
an insatiable will to express the loves we feel
in life.*

These loves are not arbitrary; we had them at birth and they have been nurtured with every tear and joy that we have experienced in life. They are our soul purpose and light the way to the very core of creation.

I CHOOSE MY
LOVES OF LIFE

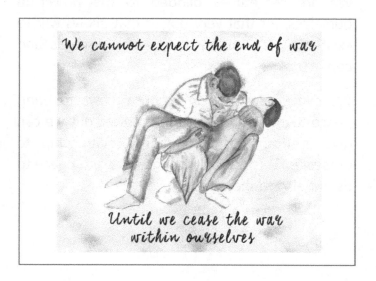

Nothing happens without the power to make it so. All that we see: the flowers of spring or the smile on a face, began first in the unseen worlds of energy. And we as humans are immense creators of it.

We are sometimes blinded to the power in ourselves, for that very power that allows war to exist comes from our own inner discords and conflicts.

We can always help in practical ways to bring peace to the world, but the greatest gift we can give is from our own caring relationship to ourselves. This not only brings light and peace to us but also to the world.

E G O

When life challenges my fragile self-view, it can unlock the box of my insecurity, releasing the tyrant of me.

This fragile ego makes me feel that who I am can be taken from me, as if I am not the author of our own life, that I am not enough. Its survival depends on not losing the 'I' of who I think I am.

So it creates a barrier between me and life to ensure that the fragile 'I' is not damaged by the world. It will name all that it sees as right or wrong, good or bad, better or worse in its attempt to separate me from life. It will evoke a sense of superiority over others to achieve this separation and if that fails, it will make me feel inferior to others; either way it will maintain the distance between 'me' and 'life'.

I can't fight the ego, only go to a place where it cannot follow

Trying to fight the ego is like going to war for peace: it's an impossible task. But I can go to places in myself where it can't go. The ego cannot see compassion, sharing or love because they mean nothing to the ego. When I am moved by these qualities it cannot follow.

THE HEART
KNOWS

THE HEART
KNOWS

WHAT THE MIND
CANNOT SEE

I do struggle to know things, to understand myself and the world I live within.

I do struggle to know things, to understand myself and the world I live within, harassing my mind to search for the truth of this and that. But the answers to the real questions of life do not exist in the head but instead within the heart.

The head and the mind are great at sorting and planning in the outer world, but they are slow, clumsy and inadequate at discerning the causal essence of life, which is always in the inner worlds. This ability is given to the heart, for it has the power and perception to see beyond the confines of our education into the world of the soul of things. And it is from the soul of things that the truth is always written.

THE FUTURE

We plant the seeds of our future with our
INTENTIONS
We create the path to our future through our
WILL
We are drawn to our future by our
ASPIRATIONS
We summon our future with our
PRAYERS
We invite our future with our
WISHES
We fix our future with our
EXPECTATIONS
We declare our future with our
LONGINGS
We picture our future with our
HOPES
We give birth to our future with our
LOVES

I am gifted with wealth of tools to make my future and I use these to create the paths and pictures that draw me forward.

The future is never fixed until I make it so, and I do this moment by moment in my life with the hundreds of attitudes I have about it each day.

I plant the seeds of my future with my INTENTIONS.

Each time my attention is in my intention it becomes another seed in my field of dreams, a reminder to myself about who I wish to be.

I create the path to my future through my WILL.

When I sharpen my mind in the light of my dream, I clear the path of the unimportant that has been made important by the absence of my will.

I am drawn to my future by my ASPIRATIONS.

The aspirations I feel are the lights from my future accomplishment showing me the way forward.

I summon our future with my PRAYERS.

The prayers I hold become the clarion call to my beloved self.

I invite my future with my
WISHES.

Each wish I create sends a thread to my future and opens the door a little wider.

I declare my future with my
LONGINGS.

My longings are drawn from the deep of me and are the song I sing to myself and the world to remind me of who I wish to be.

I picture my future with my
HOPES.

My hopes are the visions I create to paint the picture of my future; they allow the destination to be seen before I get there.

I give birth to my future with my
LOVES.

My loves are everything; they have the power to create life, to incarnate my dream into this world.

F E A R

Fear extinguishing the flame of life; it causes us to break the bonds to the heart of ourselves and so we shy away from the truth of ourselves. It drains the courage from the heart and makes us act as if we are not enough. Our expression of love becomes a pale imitation of its true colour. a muffled silence rather than the roar of our heart.

WITHIN OUR VULNERABILITY

THERE IS AN INDOMITABLE STRENGTH

I carry in my journey a fragile self that lives in the pain of what was and what was not. And I also carry a vulnerable self that is unfettered to my yesterdays. It feels the enormity of the moment without conditions or expectations of how it should be.

Do not confuse the two, for one lives in fear, the other, love.

My journey has accrued many pains that I carry forward in life; their presence gives me my sense of fragility, that I can be broken and hurt again. So I look through the eye of fear, become hard in my defence or attack against the assumed opposition to who I think I am.

This is understandable for life can be tough and is often blind to the gentle soul of ourselves. The trouble with this response is that it causes me to feel that my strength lies within my hard disposition to life. Although this can be exciting and much applauded by others in life, it is not the true strength; that strength is found in my sense of vulnerability that arises whenever I stand naked to the force of life, whenever I become unclothed by my conditions of how I think things should be. This may happen by shock or calamity or it may be purposely chosen.

Whatever the cause, I become open again to the power of life. I feel the truth of who I am, a part of all that I see; no lesser or greater than a flower or a tree, another person or a god.

My fragile self may say that I am not enough, not strong enough, not bright enough, not wise enough to accept this truth. But this is only the illusion of fear. I was, am and always will be enough.

WHAT IF

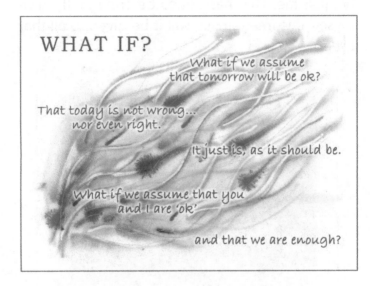

WHAT IF?

What if we assume
that tomorrow will be ok?

That today is not wrong...
nor even right.

It just is, as it should be.

What if we assume that you
and I are 'ok'

and that we are enough?

What if I give myself break, lay down my insistence on what should and should not be, relinquish my possession on tomorrow and let what is, just be what it is.

What if I assume that I am OK, not wrong or right. Or better or worse than who I was or will be, just me. That has got to be enough. If I give myself this freedom, so will it be given to all that I see.

NO GREATER LOVE

there is no greater God than in the love we share with another

What is made when two or more creators share their love becomes a life of its own, a beacon of light that does not die; it is attended and celebrated by creation because it is the purpose of creation.

We are an incredible creator of life; we create a path in life that only we can follow, creating light with the loves we feel about life. And when we do what we love it is the stuff of dreams made real – we open the chamber of our heart and life flows.

Beautiful as this is, it is only a shadow of the glory that happens when we share the love we have of life with another. When we do this, it is two universes meeting.

The light we share becomes confirmed and magnified. We graced by a purpose that is greater than who we are.

Love loves us because of our love.

NO ONE IS A NOBODY

Everybody is a somebody, with their hopes and fears, carrying their purpose for that hour, day, year along with their memories of their loves and pains.

Everybody has a mind that is searching for the peace and happiness that is worthy of the dream that they carry. They hold a thousand stories of who they are, why they are and who they will be and never stop trying to be what they love. All carry a heart that longs for nothing more than to be loved and cherished.

Everyone is a somebody, no lesser or greater than you or I.

THE PATERNAL
FATHER

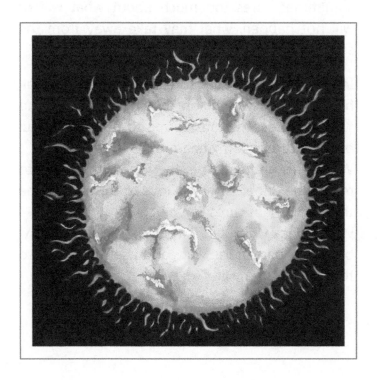

I carry within myself a paternal father who cares
deeply that I am safe in my journey. It is his duty
to make secure the heart's desire and help me
be grounded in my aspirations.

Although it is in service to the heart, he sometimes cares too much about what will or will not happen, what may take away from the safety I feel.

In trying to bring back to earth the heart's flight, he can put a weight on my shoulders, beyond what is necessary, causing me to become fearful of the future that my heart longs to fulfil.
When this happens it is the job of the heart to return the gift and give its love to this part of me that sometimes cares too much.
When I can do this, what was 'in the way' becomes 'part of the way', and I settle again into the journey of my life

WILL

The universe so loves the 'will' we create
in our journey on this earth because it is
the stuff of creation.

*We are the magician and through our Will,
we breathe life into our purpose. It is our
wand of command, and every day we choose
what we will and will not do, what we will
create and what we will resist.*

When I exercise my will I clear the path and free the mind. It is a powerful gift and not to be given away lightly. Nor is it arbitrary; it is part of the gift of life and I am its custodian.

I was not given a manual on being human or a map of how to create my heaven on earth. I have to make it myself: create the purpose, create my meaning of life and muster my heart and mind towards this end.

Every moment of every day we are exercising our will, creating and forging our path in life.

Each time I choose what meaning to give to my experience, decide what purpose the day shall have. Each time I choose what face we give to the world, who I will or will not be, I create life through my will. I can't *not* do this, for we are given an irresistible urge to never stop trying and every day I create a thousand acts to breathe life into the purpose of my life.

The universe so loves the life that our 'will' creates in our journey on this earth because it is the stuff of creation.

Each day I make hundreds of moment-by-moment decisions of what to do and how to feel. Each week I create thousands of paths in my journey of life, each month a million stories about why I am and who I am. And each year countless brush strokes have been applied to my picture of the meaning of life.

With this will power I am given the freedom to choose what to think, what meaning to give to my experience and what purpose for my actions. This power and freedom makes up my free will and it is sacrosanct. But I have surrendered much of my will in the attempt to be the things the world says I should. This is not only an impossible task but is a violation of my own will.

I reclaim my will whenever I know what I cannot live without and what I want to live for.

THE PYRE

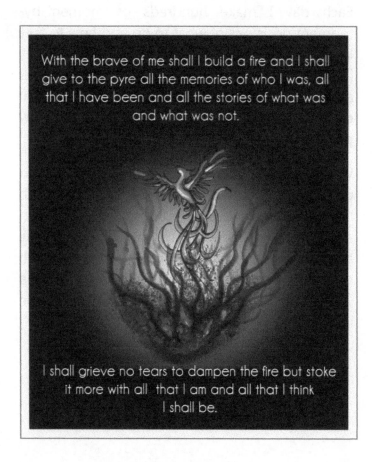

With the brave of me shall I build a fire and I shall give to the pyre all the memories of who I was, all that I have been and all the stories of what was and what was not.

I shall grieve no tears to dampen the fire but stoke it more with all that I am and all that I think I shall be.

Sometimes in life, it's great to build a fire and put upon it the weights that I carry, all the this and that, all the shoulds and shouldn'ts, all the things that were or were not, might or might not be.

This is not an easy task, it does take courage, I have to let go of the self-image I have created, and stand naked to the force of life. But the rewards are enormous; I unburden my heart, free the mind and become again a child of the universe.

I CHOOSE WHAT
I WILL DO

You don't need to know how to dance, just love dancing. You don't need to know how to paint, just love painting. You don't need to know how to sing, just love singing.

The love I feel for what I do opens the mind and the heart to more than I know; it connects me to the essence of my love and its meaning and grace flows down that connection.

When I do this, I become the champion of my love and become loved because of it.

MORE THAN WE KNOW

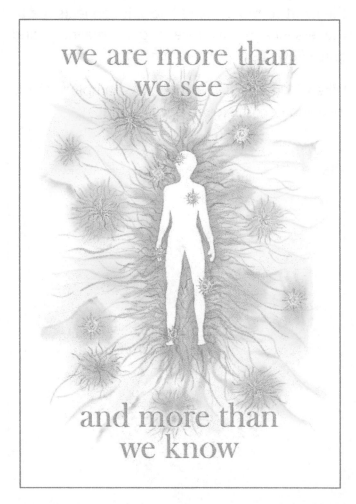

we are more than
we see

and more than
we know

We live in company with worlds that are so different to what we are led to expect, to what we are accustomed to, that they are often forgotten as phantoms of lost dreams or childish imagination. And anyway they have little to do with the real world, so we dismiss these thoughts and feelings as time wasters to the task of living. But what if these, feelings, these thoughts, these senses of worlds beyond our current perception are the real causes of life and offer us a door to worlds that make meaning, not to the world of commerce but to the soul of ourselves?

If we could see the truth of our lives, the unseen worlds that surround us, we would think ourselves a powerful piece of creation. If we could see the thousands of threads that issue from our mind to the people and things that catch our attention, if we could see the energy in the colours and pulses of the life we create every moment, if we could see the power that exists in the heart of ourselves or see the universes that we create in our cherishment of life, we would know who we really are and the profound world within which we live.

A THOUSAND THREADS

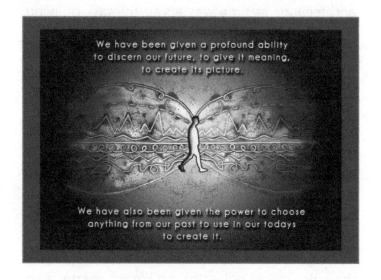

We have been given a profound ability to discern our future, to give it meaning, to create its picture.

We have also been given the power to choose anything from our past to use in our todays to create it.

Every day I create a thousand threads into my future and a thousand threads into my past that change the life I am.

I am the lord of an empire, a vast domain of resources that I can use to create my life with. I can breathe life into any purpose I wish, think anything about anything I choose, create any purpose for anything I do. There is no feeling I cannot have, no attitude I cannot muster should I seek it to be so. I also exist in a living timeline that changes according to the thoughts and feelings I have about it; every thought or feeling I send into tomorrow or give to my yesterdays changes my feeling about it and therefore changes its meaning for my life now.

I was and always will be the cause of my life. It is mine to define and in truth, I would wish it no other way.

An Emerald Prayer

help me bring the awareness of the unknown
into conscious recognition
and grant me the ability to
discern the truth in all that I see.

LIVING TIMELINE

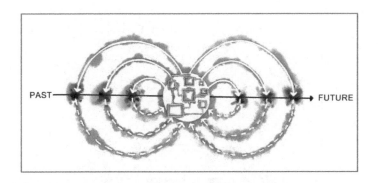

We go where our thinking goes. But what it brings back depends on why we sent it there in the first place. Be it hope, care, hostility or fear, it will set the frequency of what will and will not be returned to us.

The past is not dead nor the future unknown; it is a living timeline, changing according to our thoughts about it. We define our past and our future by how we think about them, and we can, if we have the will, change the feelings we receive from them by changing the stories we tell ourselves about who we are.

I CHOOSE WHY I DO
WHAT I DO

Each day is a lifetime of experience; a thousand, thousands things have passed my way, stirred my mind, called up memories of the past and dreams of the future.

They have poked my fears and caressed my hopes. Each day I see a hundred faces in my mind that carry their meaning of me and my meaning of them. A moment does not go by without an avalanche of life happening in me. Although I may not often see it, I know that few things have this ability that is given to the human; to experience and create. And when I go to bed, shut my eyes to the day and go to sleep, I take with me the universe I have created that day.

THE ALL OF ME

I am the all of me,
the lost of me and the found of me,
the smile of me and the frown of me,
the love of me and the fear of me.
There is nothing that happens in me that is not
me.
It seems obvious but when I really know this I
cease the war with myself,
cease to dismember myself with blame or
derision.

I become the tolerant parent to the all of me.

THE MOMENT OF
THE NOW

When we touch the moment
of the now

The universe unfolds
the heart sings and
the soul breathes in the light of freedom.

The power of life exists in the now, not in yesterday or tomorrow or even the moment yet to come.

The power of life exists in the now, not in yesterday or tomorrow or even the moment yet to come. But living in the now is a hard nut to crack because I so care what happens that I am unwilling to let life be what it is. So I put my expectations and conditions on all that happens. Although entertaining, it does separate me from the truth of the moment wherein lies the greatest treasure.

Whenever I allow myself to pause my insistence of what life should be, the universe does unfold, allowing my heart to join the stream of life. And my soul breathes again in the freedom of the moment.

be not timid
with your love

for no great life
ever happened without it

Life can sometimes make us timid in expressing our feelings. But of all things that we could be timid about, surely what we love to be and do should be given the greatest expression?

All great works are made manifest through love and passion; there is nothing of great beauty that has not been produced without it. It's a connection to a source of inspiration that lives in the very deep of us, giving us a vision of the miraculous and the power to achieve it.

Whenever we touch our loves in life, we do know that there is nothing else we would rather do, that they have all that we need to sustain the soul of ourselves. It makes life worth living and really is the purpose of life; it is the reason we are here.

The loves I feel in life light the path that only I can travel, and it is in my journey to express these that I create my heaven on earth.

THE GENTLE THREADS

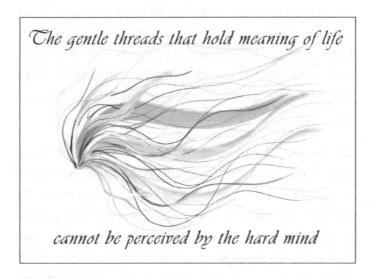

The gentle threads that hold meaning of life

cannot be perceived by the hard mind

The hard mind deals in the result, not the cause, the manifest not in the manifestor of life. It concerns itself with the physical appearance, not the essences that are the cause of life.

It can be a tough world and it seems so easy to become hard just to make a living and get by. And I am so easily drawn away from my soft mind into the hard, by the ghosts of 'more' that haunt my mind with their incessant moaning that I am not enough! This can make for a severe mind, inflexible in its purpose and with little ability to know the gentle truths that surround me.

Its not that they hide from the hard mind, it's just that there is no room in the hard mind for them to play. But I do know that when I am gentle with myself and carry few expectations of how things should be, my mind becomes flexible again and gives me knowings of a world beyond the hard lines of life, a world that is full of meanings about the purpose of life, its timeless flow and, of course, my place within it.

THE SACRED YOU

*Where are we drawn back to after the
storms in life?*

Where is it in ourselves that holds our meaning of life, our purpose, the dream we could not live without?

And how easily can we find this soul of ourselves, this place that gives peace to an aching heart.

What paths have we made, what signs have we created that allow us to see the journey home and to rejoin the conversation with our beloved self?

In learning self-love, I will,
in the end,
know that
I am a part of all creation,

no lesser or greater

than all that I see.

THE VOW

There is nothing that I see, feel or touch
that is not me.

The sea, the sun, the moon, the earth it seems are part of me, I know them, have known them for a thousand years. Somewhere in the lines of time we spoke clearly to each other; although muffled now, the vow of our communion has stood the test of time, it has not been broken and our future will not be denied. For within this unfathomable bond lies a sanctuary and a sanity.

Printed in July 2019
by Rotomail Italia S.p.A., Vignate (MI) - Italy